TRIBES of NATIVE AMERICA

Hopi

**edited by Marla Felkins Ryan
and Linda Schmittroth**

BLACKBIRCH®
PRESS

THOMSON

GALE

San Diego • Detroit • New York • San Francisco • Cleveland
New Haven, Conn. • Waterville, Maine • London • Munich

© 2003 by Blackbirch Press™. Blackbirch Press™ is an imprint of The Gale Group, Inc.,
a division of Thomson Learning, Inc.

Blackbirch Press™ and Thomson Learning™ are trademarks used herein under license.

For more information, contact
The Gale Group, Inc.
27500 Drake Rd.
Farmington Hills, MI 48331-3535
Or you can visit our Internet site at http://www.gale.com

Photo credits: Cover Courtesy of Northwestern University Library; cover © National Archives;
cover © Photospin; cover © Perry Jasper Photography; cover © Picturequest; cover © Seattle
Post-Intelligencer Collection, Museum of History & Industry; pages 5, 6, 8, 10, 11, 13, 15, 16, 17,
20, 21, 26, 28, 29, 30, 31 © CORBIS; cover, pages 7, 18, 23, 25 © Library of Congress; cover, page
7 © PhotoDisc; page 9 © Denver Public Library, Western History Collection, George Wharton
James, X-30741; page 12 © Corel Corporation; pages 14, 20 © Native Stock; page 14 © The Art
Archive; page 19 © Denver Public Library, Western History Collection, X-3077; page 22 © Denver
Public Library, Western History Collection, X-30802; page 27 © Denver Public Library, Western
History Collection, X-30783; cover, page 24 © Blackbirch Press Archives; page 24 © Steve Cohen
Travel

LIBRARY OF CONGRESS CATALOGING-IN-PUBLICATION DATA

Hopi / Marla Felkins Ryan, book edito ; Linda Schmittroth, book editor.
   v. cm. — (Tribes of Native America)
Includes bibliographical references.
Contents: Hopi name — Origins and group affiliations — Religion — Language — Daily
life — Education — Customs — Preserving the Hopi way.
  ISBN 1-56711-691-4 (alk. paper)
  1. Hopi Indians—Juvenile literature. [1. Hopi Indians. 2. Indians of North America—
Arizona.] I. Ryan, Marla Felkins. II. Schmittroth, Linda. III. Series.

E99.H7 .H683 2003
979.1004'9745—dc21
                                        2002015827

Table of Contents

HOPI

Name

Hopi is short for the tribe's original name,
Hopituh-Shi-nu-mu. It means "peaceful people."

OREGON

IDAHO

NEVADA

UTAH

COLORADO

CALIFORNIA

Hopi
Two Reservations Today
Hopi Reservation (lighter shading),
surrounded by the Navajo Nation
Reservation (darker shading)
in present-day Arizona at the Four
Corners area, where Arizona, Utah,
Colorado, and New Mexico meet

ARIZONA

NEW
MEXICO

NORTH AMERICA

Hopi

Pacific
Ocean

Gulf of
Mexico

Atlantic Ocean

Most of the 14 Hopi villages sit atop three rocky mesas in northeast Arizona.

Where are the traditional Hopi lands?

The 2.5 million-acre Hopi Reservation is in northeast Arizona. The Hopi live in 14 villages. Most are on top of three rocky mesas called First Mesa, Second Mesa, and Third Mesa. (A mesa is a high, flat area.)

What has happened to the population?

In 1680, there were about 2,800 Hopi. In a 1990 count of the population by the U.S. Bureau of the Census, 11,791 people said they were Hopi.

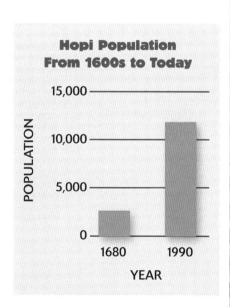

Hopi Population From 1600s to Today

Origins and group ties

The Hopi tribe has lived on its present lands for at least 1,000 years. Hopi tales say their ancestors were small creatures from another world.

The Hopi lived in pueblos like this one in Arizona in the 1400s.

The Hopi people believe they were the first to live in America. They farmed very well in their dry climate. The Hopi way of life focuses on humility, respect, and care for the earth. The Hopi have held onto much of their culture. This is in part because their homeland is isolated. They also keep their affairs secret from outsiders.

Even in the dry climate of the Southwest, the Hopi farmed very well.

HISTORY

The Hopi before contact with the Spanish

Most scholars believe people lived on the Hopi's homeland for at least 10,000 years. As long as 1,500 years ago, Hopi ancestors used technology and architecture very much like what the Hopi use today.

From 1350 to 1540, Hopi villages grew larger. Chieftains, or the heads of villages, expanded their power. At this time, kivas were first used. These were underground ceremonial chambers in all Hopi villages.

Hopi villages had underground ceremonial chambers called kivas (pictured).

The Hopi village of Oraibi (pictured) has been occupied for centuries.

By the 1550s, the Hopi culture was in place. The Hopi had a set of yearly ceremonies and a social system based on clans (groups of families that have a common ancestor). The Hopi village of Oraibi is the oldest continuously occupied settlement in the United States.

Spanish try to impose Christianity

The Hopi first met Europeans in 1540. A group of Spanish soldiers, led by Francisco Vásquez de Coronado, came to Hopi lands to look for riches. When they found no gold, they destroyed part of one Hopi village and left. The Hopi did not meet the Spanish again until 1629. That was when the first Spanish missionaries came. These Roman Catholics built missions in Oraibi and two other villages. Most Hopi pretended to adopt the new religion, but secretly kept their own.

1917–1918
WWI fought in Europe

1929
Stock market crash begins the Great Depression

1934
The Hopi Tribal Council starts to deal with Hopi–U.S. government relations

1941
Bombing at Pearl Harbor forces United States into WWII

1945
WWII ends

1950s
Reservations no longer controlled by federal government

1973
American Indian Movement (AIM) activists occupy Wounded Knee and engage in a 71-day standoff with government agents

1974
The Navajo-Hopi Settlement Act returns 900,000 acres to the Hopi

The Hopi first met Europeans when the Francisco Vásquez de Coronado expedition, depicted in this drawing, entered Hopi country in 1540 to search for gold.

The Hopi cast off Spanish rule when they joined the rest of the Pueblo people in the Pueblo Revolt of 1680. In this uprising, the Indians killed Catholic priests and Spanish soldiers in an attack on Santa Fe, New Mexico. After the battle, the Hopi went back to their villages and killed all the missionaries.

Spanish meddling ends

The Spanish returned in 1692. They took back the area near the Rio Grande, the river that separates Mexico from Texas. Many Rio Grande natives fled west to Hopi lands. They were welcomed. Over the next few years, a number of people at the Hopi village of Awatovi invited the Spanish priests back. This caused a break between those who wanted to keep the old ways and those who wanted to be Christians. Finally, in 1700, the traditional Hopi killed all the Christian men in Awatovi and then destroyed the village.

This marked the end of Spanish meddling in Hopi life. There was little more contact between the Hopi and whites until about 1850. At that time, the U.S. government sent an Indian agent to watch over the Hopi and other Indians of the region. When U.S. officials went to Hopi lands, they caused a severe smallpox epidemic. Hundreds of people died in 1853 and 1854. A drought took place soon after. The population of Oraibi dropped from 800 people to 200. When the American Civil War (1861–1865) broke out, the U.S. military left the Southwest to fight in the East. With no soldiers to stop them, the Navajo made attacks on Hopi villages. They wanted to take over Hopi land.

Hopi who were converted to Christianity by Spanish missionaries once used this church.

Navajo intrusion on Hopi land

U.S. president Chester A. Arthur knew about the Navajo attacks. In 1882, he had the Hopi Reservation set up. He gave the tribe 2.6 million acres. The way his order was worded, though, let the Navajo continue to take Hopi land for almost a century. Then, the Navajo-Hopi Indian Land Settlement Act of 1974 was passed. It gave about half of the land in question to the Hopi.

In 1950, the U.S. Congress passed the Navajo-Hopi Act. The government spent $90 million to make life on the reservation better. Roads and schools were built. Water and electricity systems were improved. In 1961, the Hopi tribal council began to lease 25,000 acres of land for mining. Since the 1960s, much less farming has been done on Hopi lands. By 1980, the main source of income was wage labor. Today, many Hopi work in coal mines and as part of the tourist trade.

A kachina is an invisible spirit that may occupy people, animals, or even lifeless objects.

Religion

The Hopi have a complex belief system. They have many gods and spirits. Among these are Earth Mother, the Sun, and the Moon. They also have many kachinas, or invisible spirits. These are found inside both living and nonliving things. Hopi religion has a yearlong schedule of rituals and

The Hopi create colorful dolls like this one for kachinas to occupy during religious rituals.

prayers. As of 1992, more than 95 percent of the people still practiced their Hopi religion.

Kivas and prayer feathers

The kiva, the paho, and the Corn Mother are important parts of Hopi religious ceremonies. The *kiva* (an underground ceremonial chamber) is usually shaped like a rectangle and sunk in the village square. It is a symbol of the place where the first Hopi people came into this world.

Dances are done in the square at the end of ceremonies inside the kiva. The *paho*, a prayer feather, is used to send prayers to the Creator. Pahos are used at all kiva ceremonies.

The *Corn Mother* is a perfect ear of corn whose tip ends in four full kernels. This ear is saved for rituals. Corn was a main food of the Hopi for centuries. It plays a large role in ceremonies.

Hopi used feathers to send prayers to the Creator.

This carving represents the Corn Mother, an important figure in Hopi religion.

For example, cornmeal is sprinkled to welcome the kachinas to the Corn Mother.

The Powamu Ceremony and Bean Dance

The Powamu Ceremony is done to ask the gods for crops. It is a 16-day series of rites that begins in February. It helps the Hopi and their dry lands get ready for the planting season. Beans are blessed and planted in moist sand. Then they are grown in kivas.

The Bean Dance celebrates the sprouting of the seeds. Kachinas dance into the village square on a path of cornmeal sprinkled by priests. The dancers stay in the village for six months. They dance to ask for rain and fertility, among other blessings.

The Crow Mother kachina walks through the village on the last day of the Powamu Ceremony. She carries a basket of fresh bean sprouts that grew

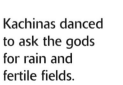

Kachinas danced to ask the gods for rain and fertile fields.

in the kiva. With the Crow Mother are her two sons, the Whipper Twins. They bare their teeth as they pretend to whip the children of the village with yucca fronds.

Hopi kachinas are said to live in the sacred San Francisco Peaks. They come to live in villages for six months of the year. Masked people dress as these spirits to do kachina dances. These are tied to the growing season, which starts in March and lasts into July.

A chief heads each Hopi village. Pictured here are Chief Loma Haftowa (left), Chief Kol Chaftowa (center), and Indian Commissioner John Collier (right) at a dedication ceremony in Washington, D.C., at the turn of the 20th century.

Government

Each Hopi village is led by a *kikmongwi*, or village chief. The Hopi villages are only loosely tied together politically. They have strong cultural ties, though.

The Hopi tribe has always used a system of clans based on the mother's family. Today, there are about 30 clans. There has been an elected Hopi Tribal Council since 1934. The council deals with matters between the Hopi and the U.S. government, but it does not run the tribe. The council is made up of a chairperson and vice president. Each of them serves a four-year term. The rest of the council members serve two-year terms.

Economy

For centuries, the Hopi stayed in one place and farmed. The men planted and harvested the crops. The women gathered other food. When a severe

Hopi men planted and harvested the crops. Farming is still a key part of the Hopi way of life.

Tourist attractions like the Hopi Cultural Center in Arizona (pictured) are important to the Hopi economy.

drought took place from 1279 to 1299, the Hopi used new farming methods that used any possible source of moisture. These techniques are still in use today.

One Hopi watering method made use of the wind. The wind blew sand up against the sides of the mesas, which formed dunes that trapped moisture. Crops were then planted in these dunes. Hopi farmers also planted in the dry washes (low ground that is sometimes flooded) as well as in the mouths of streams. At times, they watered crops by hand. Besides food crops, the Hopi also grew cotton. Men spun and wove cotton into clothing and textiles to use and to trade.

Today, small farms and ranches are a big part of the economy. A number of Hopi work to build projects such as the Hopi Industrial Park and the Hopi Water Utility Authority. Builders also work on the Hopi Cultural Center Museum and crafts shops. Places like these are in demand since tourism is very important to the Hopi economy. Visitors come to see Hopi historical sites such as Oraibi village.

DAILY LIFE

Buildings

For centuries, Hopi houses were built of local stone. The houses were set up around a village center that held one or more kivas. Today, Hopi villages are set up in much the same way.

From 1100 to 1300, the climate got drier. It was hard for farmers to grow enough food for all the people. The Hopis had to move into villages. To hold the growing population, buildings in the villages grew larger. Some had hundreds of rooms. Houses built from 1350 to 1540 were made of stone cemented with adobe (pronounced *uh-DOE-bee*; a sun-dried mud). They were very similar to the older houses of present-day Hopi.

Hopi houses like this one were built of stone and set up around a village square.

Unmarried Hopi girls wore their hair in large twists that symbolized fertility. Married women often wore braids.

Clothing

Hopi men wore fur or buckskin loincloths (flaps of material that covered the front and back and hung from the waist). The men also wove robes and blankets out of cotton. Women wore loose black gowns with a gold stripe around the waist and at the hem. Men wore shirts and loose cotton pants, covered with a blanket wrap.

Married women wore their long hair straight or in braids. Unmarried girls wore their hair in large twists on either side of the head. The shape looked like the squash blossom, a symbol of fertility. Unmarried women still wear this hairstyle today, but only for ceremonies.

Today, some Hopi women and girls still wear old-fashioned Hopi dresses. These are black and embroidered with bright red and green trim. Hopi men sometimes wear fancy outfits that use special headdresses and body paints.

Food

The main crops of the Hopi were corn, squash, and beans. They also ate some wild plants such as Indian millet and wild potato. In the 16th century, the Spanish brought wheat, onions, and new fruits to the Hopi. They also introduced chilies and mutton (sheep meat).

Many modern Hopi farmers still use the old methods. Most grow corn, melons, and many types of beans. Corn is ground for use in ceremonies. It is also used to make *piki*, a bread baked in layers on hot stones.

Hundreds of years ago, there was more wild game than there is today. Hopi men hunted deer, antelope, and elk. They also hunted rabbits with boomerangs.

Hopi women baked piki, a kind of cornbread, on hot stones.

Education

The main method to teach children Hopi ways was to speak and listen. Today, Hopi children are taught at six elementary schools, a junior high school, and a high school on the reservation. They may also go to a nearby community college.

Healing practices

Many Hopi healing methods rely on the power of suggestion. In other words, people often feel better if they believe they will soon be cured. The Hopi also know about healing plants and herbs.

There are several healing societies. Some focus on only one type of illness. For example, a snakebite would be treated by the Snake Society on First Mesa.

Some healers can suck diseases out of infants and children. To do this, they hold cornmeal in their mouth and then symbolically spit away the disease.

Many Hopi now use modern medicine. There are health clinics on the reservation and hospitals nearby.

Hopi women weave textiles (left) and make kachina dolls (right) to trade or sell.

Arts

Hopi women make fine multicolored pottery. They produce traditional textiles and handwoven baskets for trade or sale. They also make Hopi kachina dolls and ornate jewelry.

Hopi Origin Tale

Myths teach that the Hopi came from the first of Four Worlds. They were not people but insectlike creatures. Displeased with them, the Creator sent a spirit to take them on a trip. By the time they reached the Third World, they were humans. When they got to the Fourth World, they climbed up from the Underworld through a hollow reed.

In the Fourth World, the spirit Masaw gave them four stone tablets. Masaw described the travels they must take and how they would find the place they were meant to live.

This painting depicts a Hopi legend. It is divided into four parts. The number four is important in Hopi religion.

Different clans started out in each of the four directions. Their routes formed a cross. The center was the Center of the Universe, which would be their home. The number four is significant in the Hopi religion. Many rituals call for things to be repeated four times.

Hopi stories allow both children and adults to learn something new at each hearing. Each clan's stories contain information that is valuable to its members. People learn only the stories of their own clan. The Hopi consider their stories sacred and private.

CUSTOMS

Naming ceremonies

Newborn babies are kept out of the direct sun for their first 19 days. Then, a naming ceremony is held. A baby is part of its mother's clan, but it is named for the father's clan.

During the naming ritual, the baby's mother's mother kneels and washes the mother's hair. She then bathes the new baby. The grandmother rubs a mixture of water and cornmeal into the baby's hair four times. Then, each of the baby's aunts from the father's side does the same. Each gives the baby a gift and suggests a name. The grandmother chooses one of the names. Then she introduces the baby to the sun god.

Hopi babies belonged to their mother's clan but were named for their father's clan.

Some Hopi girls marked their passage into adulthood by grinding corn for four days.

Youth

Both boys and girls become part of a kachina cult between the ages of eight and ten. There are four societies—Kwan, Ahl, Tao, and Wuwutcimi. The initiation ceremony includes fasts, prayers, and a light whipping with yucca leaves.

Ten-year-old girls once took part in a ceremony in which corn was ground for a whole day at the home of the girl's father's mother. Some girls ground corn for four days to mark their first menstrual period. At that time, they also got a new name, and began to wear the squash-blossom hairstyle.

Hopi rituals are done in secret, but outsiders can watch the dances that followed the rituals.

Festivals

Hopi rituals are done in secrecy. Outsiders may sometimes watch the dances that follow, though. One of the most important Hopi ceremonies is the Soyal, the first ceremony of the year and the first kachina dance. The Niman Ceremony, or Home Dance, is the last kachina dance of the year. It gives thanks for the harvest in late July.

In the one-hour-long Snake Dance, priests handle snakes that have been brought from the desert and even put them in their mouths. At the end of the dance, the snakes are let go. This ensures that rain will come. The Snake Dance takes place every other year. In the alternate years, the Flute Dance is done. It honors the spirits of people who have died in the last two years.

Courtship and marriage

As late as 1950, courtship still used elaborate ancient customs. A bride wore a traditional white tasseled robe that was woven by her uncles. A smaller white robe was rolled up and carried. This second robe would one day serve as the woman's burial clothes. The couple lived with the mother of the bride during their first year together.

Today, a couple is often married in a church or by a town official. The bride and groom then return

Hopi priests perform the Snake Dance with live snakes to ensure rain.

Hopi brides wore a white tasseled robe that was woven by their uncles.

to the reservation. Many men no longer know how to weave, so few uncles still make the traditional robes.

Several Hopi marriage customs are still used, though. For example, the bride stays with her future in-laws for four days. During this time, she grinds corn and makes the family's meals to show that she knows how to cook. Before the wedding, the aunts of both the bride and groom have a good-natured argument. They throw mud and trade insults. Then the groom's parents ceremonially wash the couple's hair. A huge feast follows at the house of the bride's mother.

Clans still play a role in courtship. Rules discourage marriage between members of the same clan. Marriage to people outside the tribe is very rare. This has helped preserve Hopi culture.

Funerals

The Hopi religion says that the soul's trip to the land of the dead begins on the fourth day after death. As a result, bodies are buried as quickly as possible.

Any delay could make it harder for the soul to reach the underworld.

One ritual calls for a paternal aunt to wash the hair of the dead person. She then decorates the hair with prayer feathers and covers the face with a mask of raw cotton. The oldest son buries the corpse in a sitting position along with food and water. A stick is then stuck into the soil of the grave. This makes a place for the soul to leave. If rain follows, it means the soul has had a successful journey.

Land claims

The Hopi today are very concerned about land issues with the Navajo tribe. When the Hopi Reservation was first set up in 1882, nearly 2.5 million acres were put aside in northeastern Arizona. This land was for

Kachina dolls and other ritual objects decorated this kiva for a Hopi funeral.

These Hopi men marked their territory with stones after the U.S. government gave it back to them in 1986.

the Hopi and any other Indians the government might place there. The Hopi Reservation was inside a larger area that the Hopi considered their ancestral land. That larger area was given to the Navajo.

As their population increased, the Navajo expanded beyond their borders onto the Hopi Reservation. Although the Hopi complained, the government did not act. In time, the Navajo took over 1.8 million acres of Hopi land. To solve the problem, Congress passed a law in 1974 that gave 900,000 acres back to the Hopi. As late as the 1990s, though, the land dispute still continued.

Preserving Hopi culture

Hopi people are worried that the privacy surrounding their rituals has been violated. For example, stories told to visitors and photographs of rites have been published in books without permission. Observers have also taped Hopi ceremonies and sold the tapes to the public.

Notable people

Louis Tewanima (1879–1969) was a world-class
Hopi athlete. Charles Loloma (1921–1991) made
some of the world's most distinctive jewelry. Other
notable Hopi include genetic scientist Frank C.
Dukepoo (1943–), traditional artist Fred Kabotie

Hopi runner Louis
Tewanima (left)
was named to the
all-time, all-star
U.S. Olympic team
in 1954.

(c.1900–1986), award-winning artist and teacher Linda Lomahaftewa (1947–), ceramic artist Nampeyo (c.1860–1942), magazine publisher and editor Rose Robinson (1932–), poet Wendy Rose (1948–), and weaver Ramona Sakiestewa (1949–).

Hopi artist Fred Kabotie (right) created traditional Hopi paintings.

Left: Hopi potter Nampeyo was known for her ceramic work. Right: Ramona Sakiestewa gained fame for her weaving.

For More Information

Benedek, Emily. *The Wind Won't Know Me: A History of the Navajo-Hopi Land Dispute.* New York: Knopf, 1992.

Indian Reservations: *A State and Federal Handbook.* Compiled by the Federation of American Indians. Jefferson, NC: McFarland and Company, 1986.

Kavasch, E. Barrie. *Enduring Harvests: Native American Foods and Festivals for Every Season.* Old Saybrook, CT: The Globe Pequot Press, 1995.

Leitch, Barbara A. *A Concise Dictionary of Indian Tribes of North America.* Algonac, MI: Reference Publications, Inc., 1979.

Page, Susanne, and Jake Page. *Hopi.* New York: Harry Abrams, 1982.

Parsons, Elsie Clews. *Hopi and Zuñi Ceremonialism.* New York: Harper and Bros., 1950. Reprint. Millwood, NY: Kraus Reprint, 1976.

Glossary

Kivas underground ceremonial chambers

Peyote a drug used in certain religious practices that may give the user visions

Raid an attack on land or a settlement, usually to steal food and other goods

Reservation land set aside and given to Native Americans

Ritual something that is custom or done in a certain way

Tribe a group of people who live together in a community

Index